INTERACTIVE
PROJECTS & DISPLAYS
Ideas for a **Student-Created** Learning Environment

Written by
Nicole Groeneweg

We love our classroom
because we helped make it!

Editor: Stacey Faulkner
Illustrator: Jane Yamada/Stick Kids by Raquel Herrera
Designers: Moonhee Pak and Barbara Peterson
Cover Designer: Barbara Peterson
Art Director: Moonhee Pak
Project Director: Sue Lewis

Table of Contents

Introduction

Take a moment to look around your classroom. Is it rich with print? Does it reflect your students' knowledge? Is the curriculum displayed so that children are drawn into the learning environment? And most importantly, have the children participated in creating the materials that contribute to their classroom community?

Successful learners emerge from classrooms where teachers have included the children in the process of constructing meaning and making connections. The activities in *Interactive Projects and Displays* provide teachers opportunities to include children in the creation of their own learning tools and resources, and give them ownership of their learning community.

Featured Sections

In Every Classroom

Children create a classroom alphabet, birthday chart, nameplates, number lines, and more. These resources are an integral part of primary classrooms and support daily learning.

Daily Morning Routines

Begin each day with routines that are fundamental in a well-managed morning meeting. Children help write the morning message, make calendar dates, weather charts, and other items used during the morning class meeting.

Anchor Charts

Use these to enhance instruction and provide readily available references that aid children in working independently. Children's contributions are a vital component in the creation of these charts.

Language Arts and Comprehension Strategies

This section provides activities to strengthen the reading-writing connection. Ideas for making words, learning about parts of speech, making connections with text, and asking questions to enhance comprehension are included.

Hands-on Math

Children participate in interactive math lessons and use manipulatives to enhance their learning. Place many of the lessons at the math center for continued reinforcement.

Bulletin Boards and Displays with Curricular Connections

Children demonstrate their learning and showcase their work in these creative, engaging bulletin boards and displays. Activities for all content areas are included.

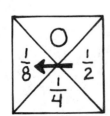

Learning Games

What's more fun than playing games? Children create their own games to reinforce concepts they are learning. Science, geography, math, and language skills are spotlighted.

How to Use This Book

The activities in *Interactive Projects and Displays* are grouped by related categories and listed in the section introductions. Use the activities as designed or adapt them to a particular season, to a theme you are studying, or to the varying skill levels of your students to meet the needs of your classroom. Every activity in this resource includes the following:

- Description of the activity and its educational value
- List of the academic standards and student learning objectives covered
- Complete list of materials
- Explicit instructions for implementing the activity
- Examples of authentic work for visual references

Use this resource to enhance student learning and give further meaning to the classroom community. At the beginning of the school year, or before a new unit of study, look around the classroom and imagine the learning environment that you and your students will help create.

Meeting Standards

Interactive Projects and Displays enables you to teach creatively and cover academic standards. Use the *Standards Check* and *Children Will* sections to identify the standards and specific learning objectives for each activity. Together, these sections allow you to demonstrate the skills being addressed.

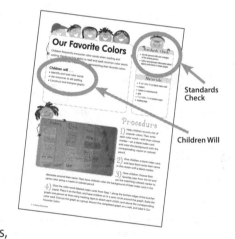

Standards Check

Children Will

Helpful Tips and Resources

Many of the activities require materials that are traditionally available in most schools. A few call for inexpensive items, such as colored sticker dots and plastic confetti. Teacher supply stores, local dollar stores, yard sales, and parent volunteers are often good resources. Laminating work, using fadeless craft paper, card stock, and tagboard-weight chart paper will enhance the resilience and durability of many activities and help your students' created work last longer.

Meeting Standards

Because standards vary, we have adapted standards from McREL for use in our standards chart. McREL has been a nationally recognized leader in standards-based education for more than a decade. For more information on McREL, visit their website at www.mcrel.org

Mid-continent Research for Education and Learning
4601 DTC Blvd. Suite 500
Denver, CO 80237
303-337-0990

Activity Titles	**Language Arts** — Use grammatical and mechanical conventions in written work	Use descriptive words to convey basic ideas	Gather and use information for research purposes	Use the general skills and strategies of the reading process	Understand and interpret a variety of literary texts	Understand and interpret a variety of informational texts	Use listening and speaking strategies for different purposes	**Math** — Use a variety of strategies in the problem-solving process	Use basic and advanced properties of number concepts	Use basic and advanced procedures to perform computation	Use basic and advanced properties of measurement concepts	Use basic and advanced properties of geometry concepts	Collect and represent information about objects or events in simple graphs	Recognize regularities in designs, shapes, and sets of numbers/extend simple patterns	**Science** — Understand atmospheric processes	Understand relationships among organisms and their physical environment	Understand the nature of scientific inquiry	**Geography** — Understand the characteristics and uses of maps and globes	Understand the concept of regions
Classroom Alphabet	●			●															
Happy Birthday to You!													●						
How We Get Home				●									●						
Our Favorite Colors	●												●						
Nameplates																			
Number Lines									●		●								
Big Book of Routines							●												
Morning Message	●			●			●												
Venn Diagram							●						●						
Calendar Patterns														●					
Weather Charts															●				
Portable Word Walls	●			●															
Alphabet Pockets				●															
Vivid Vowels	●			●															
Illustrated Word Patterns	●			●															
Vocabulary Charts	●			●															
What Good Readers Do				●			●												
What Good Writers Do				●			●												

Create a Word

Parts of Speech Big Books

Linking Connections

Questions, Anyone?

Nonfiction Facts

A Picture in Your Mind

Synthesizing Puzzles

Strategies Minifolder

Classroom Book Nook

Bugs on Leaves

Open Wide for Subtraction

Daily Number Spotlight

Fact Family Magnets

Magic In and Out Box

Leaf Arrays

Mystery Addend Cards

Secret Numbers

Clockworks

Folding Yardsticks

Decorated Tree Combinations

Garden Plot

Group Inventories

Math Kits

Instead of Said

Measuring Sunflowers

Interpreting Graphs

Data Retrieval Charts

Diurnal/Nocturnal Folders

Pollinating Bees

A Slice of Pizza

What's the Buzz?

The Cinderella Game

Water World

In Every Classroom

Integral Classroom Resources That Support Daily Learning

Winter — mber January February

Spring — March April May

Summer — June July Augu

Happy Birthday to You!

Contents

Classroom Alphabet

Alphabet letter cards are a staple in every primary classroom. Give children the opportunity to make a contribution to their class on the very first day of school by participating in the creation of their own classroom alphabet. Change the alphabet throughout the year according to themes. Bind previous alphabets into books for the reading center.

Children will . . .

• Brainstorm a list of words for each letter of the alphabet
• Use basic elements of phonetic analysis to decode and spell words

Procedure

1) Have children brainstorm words that begin with each letter of the alphabet and record these words on chart paper.

2) Assign each child a different letter of the alphabet. Give children a corresponding upper- and lowercase alphabet letter and the white construction paper. Have children glue the letters in the upper left corner of their paper.

3) Ask children to choose one or two words from the list that begin with the same sound as their letter. Have children use markers to illustrate a picture that includes their chosen words. Encourage children to color the background as well. Have children use blank address labels to write their words and match them to their illustrations. Mount the alphabet cards on the black construction paper and hang them above the white board.

Happy Birthday to You!

Discussing and sharing children's birthdays is an excellent way to make connections, strengthen classroom community, and teach math and science concepts. This child-created birthday graph is guaranteed to be a staple used throughout the year!

Children will . . .

• Match months to seasons
• Create "real" graphs and picture graphs
• Graph their birthday dates
• Compare and interpret information on a graph

Standards Check

◄ Collect and represent information about objects and events in simple graphs

Materials

◄ construction paper in assorted colors
◄ 4 pieces of blue poster board
◄ sentence strips
◄ 8" (20 cm) child-shaped card stock tracers
◄ scissors
◄ glue
◄ markers or crayons

Autumn   Winter   Spring   Summer

Procedure

1) Prepare in advance the backdrops your graphs will be mounted on. Use construction paper to create labels for each season, attach them to each piece of poster board, and set aside.

2) Write the names of the months on sentence strips. Ask children to order the months, and discuss seasonal groupings. Have children brainstorm seasonal characteristics, and record their ideas for later use. Place the sentence strips across the floor, in order, beginning with January. Have children stand in lines behind their birthday months in a "real" graph and discuss the results.

3) Ask children to use a child-shaped tracer, construction paper, and markers or crayons to create figures of themselves for the graph. Remind them to use the seasonal characteristics from Step 2 as they "dress" their figures. Have children make a balloon for recording their name and birth date.

4) As children are working, attach the sentence strips created in Step 2 to the poster boards. Help children glue their figures and balloons to the graph in the correct month and order of birth dates. Discuss the graph as a class.

How We Get Home

Transportation is a common primary theme. Have children create a *How We Get Home* chart to strengthen your classroom community during the first week of school. Children won't miss the bus again, or forget how they are getting home, when everyone can use the chart to support one another. This handy chart can also be used to aid substitute teachers at the end of the school day!

Children will . . .
- Use a chart to organize information
- Discuss and interpret information found on a chart

Standards Check
◄ Collect and represent information about objects and events in simple graphs

Materials
◄ library card pockets
◄ permanent markers—black and colored
◄ glue
◄ craft sticks
◄ poster board

Procedure

1) Discuss with the children the different ways they go home from school each day—walk, childcare buses, school buses, or automobiles.

2) Label library card pockets with the different modes of transportation. Be sure to make separate pockets for each of the different bus routes.

3) Ask volunteers to illustrate library pockets to represent the various ways they go home from school. Glue the library pockets along the bottom edge of the poster board. Label the chart *How We Get Home.*

4) Have children use black permanent markers to write their names on craft sticks and use the colored permanent markers to decorate the background. Ask children to place their craft sticks in the pocket depicting the way they go home. Discuss the chart as a group. Compare the numbers of children going home by different methods. Place the chart in a spot easily accessible by children and substitute teachers.

Our Favorite Colors

Children frequently encounter color words when reading and writing. Reinforce their ability to read and spell common color words by having children create a graph representing their favorite colors.

Children will . . .

- Identify and read color words
- Use resources to aid spelling
- Construct and interpret graphs

Standards Check

- Use the general skills and strategies of the reading process
- Collect and represent information about objects and events in simple graphs

Materials

- 4" x 6" (10 x 15 cm) blank index cards
- markers
- crayons or colored pencils
- glue
- 3' x 4' (0.9 x 1.2 m) butcher paper
- masking tape

Procedure

1) Help children record a list of popular colors. Then write each color word—with that colored marker—on a blank index card and color the background with the corresponding crayon or colored pencil.

2) Give children a blank index card, and have them write their name in the center with a black marker.

3) Have children choose their favorite color from the list and use the matching colored marker to decorate around their name. Then have children color the background of their index card in the same color using a crayon or colored pencil.

4) Glue the color-word-labeled index cards from Step 1 along the bottom edge of the butcher paper. Place it on the floor, and have children sit in a semi-circle around the graph. Build the graph one person at a time using masking tape to attach each child's card above the corresponding color card. Discuss the graph as a group. Mount the completed graph on a wall, and label it *Our Favorite Colors*.

Materials

◄ nameplate reproducible (page 66)
◄ thin-tipped black markers
◄ colored markers
◄ contact paper

Nameplates

Nameplates are handy and useful resources that are right at children's fingertips. Children love having their own personalized space in the classroom! Have children create their own customized nameplates, designed to meet their individual needs or the needs of your class.

Children will . . .

• Practice correct letter and numeral formation
• Practice alphabet skills and number line skills
• Use resources to aid spelling
• Create a hands-on resource for color words, shapes, and other common concepts

Procedure

1) Review basic handwriting skills, and then have children use markers to write their name using the handwriting line provided. Encourage children to use upper- and lowercase letters correctly.

2) Review the classroom alphabet, and have children add both upper- and lowercase letters to the nameplate. Have children write the letters in pencil so that any needed corrections can be made. Ask children to trace over their letters using a black marker.

3) Review numbers 1–20 on the class number line, and have children write them on the number line on their nameplate. Follow the same procedure as in Step 2 to support correct numeral formation.

4) Choose one important concept, such as shape words, that you would like children to add above the number line on their nameplate. Have children write the shape word next to a corresponding shape. Attach nameplates to desks using contact paper.

Number Lines

Counting on and counting back to add and subtract numbers are two essential computational strategies. Becoming efficient with these strategies becomes much easier with these child-made number lines! Alternating colored dots will help children easily identify even and odd numbers.

Children will . . .

- Create a number line with evenly marked 1" (2.5 cm) segments
- Identify even and odd numbers
- Use the strategies of counting on and counting back
- Use their number line to solve addition and subtraction number sentences

Standards Check

◄ Use basic and advanced properties of measurement concepts
◄ Use basic and advanced properties of number concepts

Materials

◄ sentence strips
◄ yardsticks or meter sticks
◄ markers
◄ sticker dots in two different colors

Procedure

1) Have children use a yardstick or meter stick to mark 21 evenly spaced 1" (2.5 cm) segments on the single-lined side of a sentence strip.

2) Assist children in placing dots on the lines at the marked intervals in alternating colors.

3) Have children write numerals 0–20 in consecutive order on the dots.

4) Laminate number lines, and place them at children's desks or at the math center. Let children use overhead markers or grease pencils to mark the number lines when counting on or counting back.

Materials

◄ chart paper
◄ camera
◄ 15" x 20" (38 x 51 cm) poster board
◄ markers
◄ book rings

Big Book of Routines

Each classroom operates with its own unique routines and procedures. Create a *Big Book of Routines* to reinforce the routines and procedures established during the first weeks of school. Use this resource as a way to establish continuity with substitute teachers.

Children will . . .
• Practice routines and procedures
• Communicate through shared writing

Procedure

1) At the end of the first week of school, or anytime after that, have children brainstorm a list of classroom routines, procedures, and any important aspects of the class. Examples include morning circle time activities, classroom centers, daily routines, class motto, and class behavior procedures. Record their ideas on chart paper.

2) Photograph the children during the day participating in classroom routines and visiting specialists or other important staff members. Be sure to take photos of any ideas brainstormed by the children.

3) Group photographs by topic and attach them to poster board. During a shared writing activity, record children's descriptions of the photos on the poster board. Each poster becomes a page for the book.

4) Use book rings to bind each page into a book and place it in the reading center. Remember to include notes in the lesson plans to direct substitute teachers to this resource.

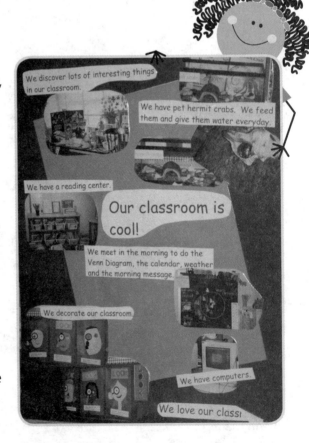

Daily Morning Routines

Routines for a Well-Managed Morning Meeting

Morning Message

Contents

Materials

◀ chart paper
◀ markers
◀ pointer

Morning Message

Model appropriate writing and incorporate writing mini-lessons into meaningful text with a daily morning message. Children love sharing their experiences with the class, so let them write the message through this interactive writing activity!

Children will . . .

• Communicate through a shared writing of the morning message

• Identify correct use of punctuation, capitalization, and quotation marks

• Use knowledge of plurals and possessives

• Participate in a shared reading of the morning message

Procedure

1) Write the date at the top of the chart paper in green. Invite children to share personal experiences, such as *My friend came over to my house last night,* or *I lost another tooth and it hurt!* Record their words in blue. Do not include any punctuation at this time.

2) As children share, ask them to use words describing "how'" something was said. For example, *"My friend came over to my house last night!" shouted Mark.* Or *Molly moaned, "I lost another tooth and it hurt."*

3) Ask speakers to come to the chart and use a red marker to add the missing punctuation for their sentence. Model and support the children through this process at the beginning of the year. Continue with three or four children or until the chart is full. Culminate the activity with a shared reading of the morning message.

Optional: Use the morning message for a variety of writing mini-lessons on capital letters, word endings, prefixes, plurals, or possessives.

Venn Diagram

This oversized hands-on graphic organizer will support children's understanding of gathering and sorting information, and serve as a record of daily attendance. It is an effective tool for your morning meeting.

Children will . . .

- Answer questions to gather and sort information on a Venn diagram
- Create a visual representation of information
- Use the Venn diagram to interpret information

Standards Check

- ◄ Collect and represent information about objects and events in simple graphs
- ◄ Use listening and speaking strategies for different purposes

Materials

- ◄ 2" (5 cm) multicultural construction paper circles
- ◄ construction paper in assorted colors
- ◄ markers
- ◄ scissors
- ◄ glue
- ◄ self-adhesive magnets
- ◄ 2 magnetized grouping hoops

Procedure

1) Give each student a multicultural construction paper circle. Invite children to make models of their own face and add details with construction paper and markers. Laminate the faces and add magnets to the backs. Make sure to create your own face too.

2) In advance, purchase grouping hoops from a local teacher supply store. Overlap the grouping hoops on a magnetic board. Label each hoop with a statement, for example, *has a pet* and *likes ice cream*. As the children become familiar with this routine, they can begin naming the sets.

3) Use a think-aloud to model for children the process of deciding where to place your own construction paper face on the diagram. Provide this support until children are comfortable completing the activity independently.

4) Call small groups of children up to place their faces on the Venn diagram (groups may be called by tables, birthday months, or colors worn).

5) After the children have placed their faces into the diagram, discuss the information learned.

Standards Check

◄ Recognize regularities in designs, shapes, and sets of numbers/extend simple patterns

Materials

◄ 3" x 3" (7.5 x 7.5 cm) squares of black construction paper
◄ construction paper in assorted colors
◄ scissors
◄ glue
◄ markers
◄ hole punches
◄ 1" (2.5 cm) number squares 1–31
◄ class calendar

The calendar is an integral part of morning meetings in the primary classroom and offers many opportunities to teach math skills, including patterning. Children will love predicting the next day's pattern when they have helped make the calendar dates! This morning routine provides opportunity for rich discussion of patterning vocabulary.

Children will . . .

• Recognize, describe, and extend a wide variety of patterns
• Discover pattern stems of repeating patterns
• Identify growing patterns
• Expand mathematical vocabulary

Procedure

1) Invite children to select a theme for the calendar based on the month.

2) Give each child 3 black construction paper squares. Ask each child to make snowmen pictures on the squares, one with no snowflakes, one with six snowflakes, and one with ten snowflakes. Have children use a hole punch to create snowflakes. By asking each child to create 3 pictures, you will have more than enough cards to make different patterns.

3) Secretly arrange the finished pictures in a pattern according to the number of snowflakes in the picture. These patterns can be repeating or growing and should be varied from month to month. After the pattern is complete add numbers in the corners of the pictures to complete the calendar dates and laminate. Keep the pictures you did not use for children to pattern at a math center.

4) Each morning, ask children to predict what the picture will be before adding the date. Have children name and describe the type of pattern being created.

Weather Charts

Children are naturally curious about seasonal changes and weather. Have children create and illustrate the weather chart to be used in the class's morning meeting. Recording the weather each day can lead to an increased understanding of local weather changes.

Children will . . .
- Monitor weather changes on a daily basis
- Investigate seasonal weather changes
- Write and illustrate weather words
- Create a weather chart

Standards Check
- Understand atmospheric processes

Materials
- chart paper
- 15" (38 cm) white poster board circles
- markers
- card stock
- teardrop-shaped tracers
- hole punches
- brass fasteners

Procedure

1) Label four pieces of chart paper *Autumn*, *Winter*, *Spring*, and *Summer*. Brainstorm seasonal characteristics for each season with the class, and record their ideas on the appropriate chart.

2) In advance, cut out a poster board circle for each child and divide it into eight equal sections. Ask children to choose two seasonal words from each chart created in Step 1. Have children illustrate and label the eight words on the individual sections of poster board, and then have them use a thick black marker to outline each section.

3) Provide children with card stock and a teardrop-shaped tracer to create a pointer. Ask children to label it *Today's Weather*. Show children how to hole-punch the rounded end of the pointer and use a brass fastener to attach it to their weather chart. Cut a small slit in the center of each weather chart to make it easier for children to attach their pointer.

4) Change the weather charts weekly to rotate the children's work.

Anchor Charts

References to Enhance Instruction and Aid Children in Working Independently

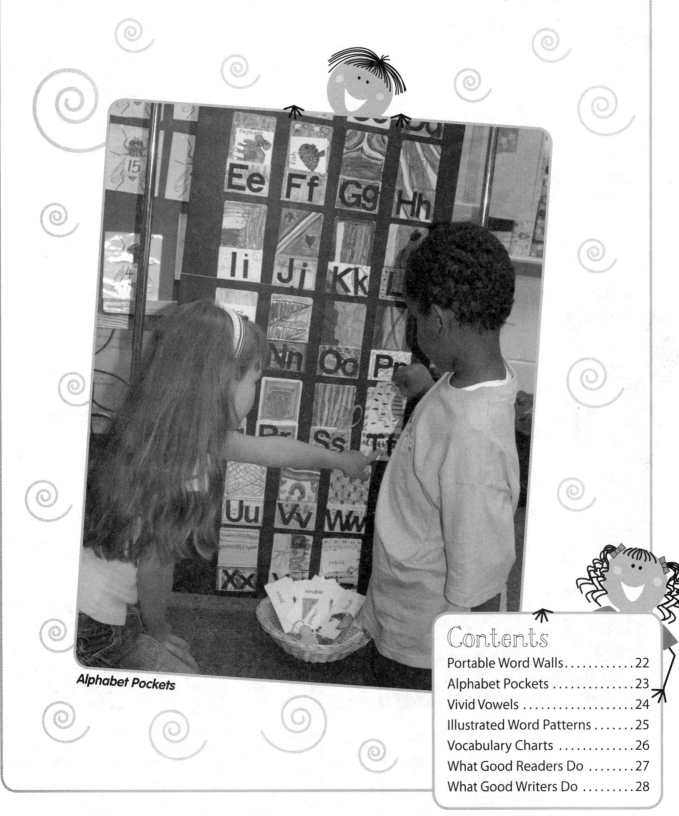

Alphabet Pockets

Contents

Portable Word Walls

Portable word walls provide flexibility in adding words during any activity. Use them for small group or outdoor lessons, and use your extra wall space to hang children's work. These user-friendly, child-size charts will make spelling a breeze!

Children will . . .
• Choose words to add to word walls
• Use basic elements of phonetic analysis to decode and spell words
• Use resources to aid spelling
• Alphabetize word charts

Standards Check

◄ Use grammatical and mechanical conventions in written work
◄ Use the general skills and strategies of the reading process

Materials

◄ picture cards of animals or objects matching each alphabet letter
◄ 6" x 12" (15 x 30.5 cm) construction paper rectangles
◄ glue
◄ chart paper
◄ scissors
◄ tape
◄ markers
◄ small plastic-coated wire hangers
◄ chart stand

Procedure

1) Find pictures of animals or objects whose names begin with each letter of the alphabet. You will need two pictures for each letter. Add upper- and lowercase letters to each picture. Mount these on the construction paper rectangles to create alphabet headers for your portable word wall.

2) Cut chart paper into thirds vertically. Attach a piece of chart paper to the bottom of an alphabet header created in Step 1. Then tape the piece of construction paper onto a hanger. Do this for each letter of the alphabet. Hang the portable word walls on a chart stand.

3) Introduce the portable word wall, and add words as needed. Encourage children to use the portable word wall charts as a resource when writing. Remind children to keep charts on the stand in alphabetical order.

Standards Check

◄ Use the general skills and strategies of the reading process

Materials

◄ cutout alphabet letters and blends
◄ 28 library card pockets
◄ markers
◄ glue
◄ foam core display board
◄ small objects and magazine pictures
◄ basket

Alphabet Pockets

Help reluctant or struggling readers and writers learn alphabet sounds with this interactive display board! Children will sort small items or pictures into library pockets labeled with the corresponding sounds. Children can add new items or pictures to be sorted as they learn new sounds.

Children will . . .

• Identify beginning sounds of objects and pictures
• Match letters to their sounds
• Learn letter-sound relationships

Procedure

1) Have students glue a different letter (upper- and lowercase) onto each library card pocket and use markers to decorate the card. Glue library card pockets to a display board.

2) Fill a basket with small items such as tiny plastic animals or toy cars, a ring, a pencil, and scissors. Also place in the basket small magazine cutouts depicting various items.

3) Place the basket with the display board at a center for children to sort the items into the library pockets according to the beginning sounds of each object or picture.

Optional: Add pockets for letter blends, or have children sort by ending sounds.

Vivid Vowels

Vowel sounds are difficult for children to learn and distinguish from one another. Help bring vowels to life with these large vowel posters. Children will use these posters as resources for their own writing.

Children will . . .

- Brainstorm words containing short and long vowels
- Identify short and long vowel sounds
- Use short and long vowel sounds to decode and spell unfamiliar words
- Learn spelling rules for short and long vowels

Standards Check

- Use grammatical and mechanical conventions in written work
- Use the general skills and strategies of the reading process

Materials

- poster board—one color for each vowel letter
- scissors
- sentence strips
- markers
- magazines (optional)

Procedure

1) Cut out a large block letter *a* shape from poster board. Write *short a* on a sentence strip, and attach it to the letter poster as a label.

2) Have children brainstorm words containing the short *a* sound and record them on the vowel-shaped poster. Invite children to underline the vowel in each word they share.

3) Use the words on the charts to discuss spelling rules.

4) Follow the procedure above for all of the vowel sounds. Match the color of the short and long vowel posters (e.g., short *a* and long *a* in blue, short *e* and long *e* in red). Remember to include *y* as a vowel.

Optional: Make small vowel-shaped booklets in the same colors as the vowel posters. Have children record words and illustrate them using markers or pictures from magazines.

Standards Check

◀ Use grammatical and mechanical conventions in written work
◀ Use the general skills and strategies of the reading process

Materials

◀ chart paper
◀ scissors
◀ markers
◀ hooked clothespins
◀ chart stand

Illustrated Word Patterns

Recognizing patterns in words aids decoding and spelling. When children are involved in creating lists of words that have meaning to them, they will be more likely to use the lists as a resource in their daily writing. Hang these lists on a chart stand with hooked clothespins to provide easy access for young writers.

Children will . . .

- Brainstorm lists of words containing specific word patterns
- Use word patterns to decode and spell unfamiliar words

Procedure

1) Choose a weekly word-family pattern (e.g., *-at, -in, -ake*). Cut chart paper into thirds vertically to use for your word lists. Label the top of each chart with the chosen pattern.

2) As a class or in small groups, brainstorm a list of words that belong to the word-family pattern. Record the list on chart paper. Use one color marker for the word-family pattern and another color for the rest of the letters.

3) Have children illustrate some of the words on the list. Read the list as a group.

4) Use hooked clothespins to hang lists on a chart stand for future reference. Repeat this procedure each week by focusing on a different word-family pattern.

Vocabulary Charts

Use child-created vocabulary charts to connect content areas with writing and help expand children's vocabulary. Keep these vocabulary lists handy for review throughout the year. You're guaranteed to see the new vocabulary used in children's writing when they have easy access to these charts.

Children will . . .

- List words specific to subject areas and topics of study
- Use resources to aid spelling
- Expand vocabulary

Procedure

1) Cut chart paper into thirds vertically to use for your word lists. Label individual charts with content areas or topics of study. Have charts available during your math, science, or thematic study time so that you can easily record new vocabulary.

2) Invite children to illustrate some of the words on the chart.

3) Use hooked clothespins to hang vocabulary charts from a chart stand.

Suggestions for vocabulary chart titles include *Words Mathematicians Use, Words Scientists Use, Words We See in Fairy Tales, Weather Words, Desert Terminology,* and *Ocean Vocabulary.*

Standards Check

- Use listening and speaking strategies for different purposes
- Use the general skills and strategies of the reading process

Materials

- 1½' x 6' (0.5 x 1.8 m) butcher paper
- markers
- scissors

What Good Readers Do

Children demonstrate greater understanding when they can verbalize their own thinking. Since children are the creators of this anchor chart, they will be sure to refer to it when they are reading independently. Teachers can use the chart to point out specific strategies during guided reading lessons, thereby reinforcing good reading practice.

Children will . . .

- Use prior knowledge to generate a list of what good readers do
- Use resources to aid decoding and comprehension strategies

Procedure

1) Use light-colored butcher paper to make a bookmark-shaped chart. Label the chart *What Good Readers Do*. Laminate the chart.

2) After several mini-lessons on this topic, ask children *What do good readers do?* Record their responses on the chart with a permanent marker. Prompt children to include such ideas as *make predictions*, *ask questions while reading*, *make connections to the story*, and *use a variety of strategies to figure out words*.

3) Create this chart in one sitting or add to it as mini-lessons are taught. At the end of the year, simply use a cleaning agent such as rubbing alcohol or hair spray to erase the permanent marker, and reuse the chart the following year.

What Good Writers Do

Because children's input is integral to the creation of this chart, they are sure to use it frequently during writing time. The chart will serve as a reference for good writing strategies that children can use to create writing goals, or use as a checklist when editing or revising.

Children will . . .

- Use prior knowledge to generate a list of the strategies that good writers use
- Use resources to aid knowledge of writing conventions and strategies

Standards Check

◄ Use listening and speaking strategies for different purposes
◄ Use the general skills and strategies of the reading process

Materials

◄ yellow butcher paper
◄ pink construction paper
◄ manila paper
◄ scissors
◄ glue
◄ permanent marker

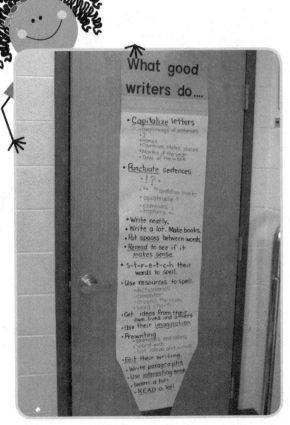

Procedure

1) Use yellow butcher paper to make a pencil-shaped chart. Use pink paper to create an "eraser" and manila paper to represent the wooden tip of the pencil. Label the chart *What Good Writers Do*. Laminate the chart.

2) After several mini-lessons on this topic, ask children *What do good writers do?* Record their responses on the chart with a permanent marker. Responses could include ideas such as *choose interesting words, use correct punctuation,* and *use resources to help spell words.*

3) Create this chart in one sitting or add to it as mini-lessons are taught. At the end of the year, simply use a cleaning agent such as rubbing alcohol or hair spray to erase the permanent marker, and reuse the chart the following year.

Language Arts and Comprehension Strategies
Ideas to Strengthen the Reading–Writing Connection

Questions, Anyone?

Contents

Create a Word

Increase the effectiveness of your phonics and spelling instruction by relating it to what children are learning about in the classroom. Provide magnetic letters and metal cookie sheets to create a hands-on experience that will help children identify patterns in words and become better spellers.

Children will . . .
- Manipulate letter sounds, blends, and word chunks to make words
- Apply knowledge of letter-sound relationships to spell new words
- Work with words to develop knowledge of prefixes and suffixes

Standards Check
- Use grammatical and mechanical conventions in written work
- Use the general skills and strategies of the reading process

Materials
- magnetized alphabet letters
- metal cookie sheets
- chart paper
- markers
- 8 ½" x 11" (21.5 x 28 cm) copy paper
- stapler

Procedure

1) In advance, gather multiples of each magnetic letter. Have children manipulate the magnetized letters on cookie sheets to create new words from *UNDER THE SEA* or any other thematic phrase.

2) Encourage children to think of sight words, word families, adding *s* to make plurals, and word endings to make words such as *rat, sat, hat, rats, hats, these,* and *heated.*

3) Record the child-created words on a chart labeled *UNDER THE SEA.*

Optional: Create recording booklets by folding three pieces of copy paper in half horizontally. Staple along the folded edge. Have children title their booklet *Under the Sea.* Invite children to choose ten of their favorite words to write in sentences and illustrate.

Parts of Speech Big Books

Knowing the basic parts of speech can enhance children's writing. Make learning about parts of speech fun and easy by having children create individual pages for nouns, verbs, or adjectives. Compiled into big books, these pages become valuable resources in the writing center.

Children will . . .

• Learn the definitions and uses of nouns, verbs, and adjectives
• Brainstorm a list of nouns, verbs, and adjectives
• Write and illustrate sentences with nouns, verbs, and adjectives

Procedure

1) Cut unlined chart paper into fourths to create the pages for your book. Gather the class together and brainstorm a list of verbs. Write these on a chart labeled *Verbs*.

2) Have each child choose a word from the list to use in a sentence and illustrate on the chart paper. Bind these pages into a book titled *Verbs*. Have children write the word they chose for their page on the title page.

3) Place the big book in the writing center as a reference. Challenge children to find new words from their reading to add new pages to the *Verbs* big book.

4) Follow the same procedure to create similar books for nouns and adjectives.

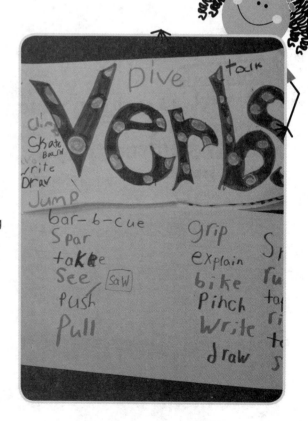

Linking Connections

Making connections with text strengthens comprehension. Capitalize on children's love for sharing personal experiences while demonstrating how making connections can lead to a better understanding of stories. Use this activity with any book related to the reading curriculum or topic being studied.

Children will . . .

- Make text-to-self and text-to-text connections
- Use comprehension strategies when reading

Standards Check

- ◄ Understand and interpret a variety of literary texts
- ◄ Use grammatical and mechanical conventions in written work

Materials

- ◄ Suggested book:
  Olivia . . . and the Missing Toy by Ian Falconer (Atheneum Books)
- ◄ 4" x 6" (10 x 15 cm) white construction paper rectangles
- ◄ 8" (20 cm) diameter black construction paper circles
- ◄ 4" (10 cm) diameter construction paper circles in all colors
- ◄ markers and glue
- ◄ 1 ½" x 12" (4 x 30.5 cm) construction paper strips in assorted colors

Procedure

1) Divide a chart into two sections and label them, *Text-to-Self*, and *Text-to-Text Connections*. Read aloud *Olivia and the Missing Toy*. During the reading, stop and record connections children are making in the appropriate column.

2) Give each child a white construction paper rectangle, two black construction paper circles, and one colored construction paper circle. Ask children to use markers to recreate the cover of the story on the white paper and glue it to one of the black circles. Then have children write *I Understand the Story* on the colored paper circle and glue it onto the second black circle. Set these pieces aside.

3) Give children six paper strips. Ask children to recall connections they made to the story and write each one on a different strip.

4) Make a slit near the edge of the black circle that has the book cover attached. Help children slide the first strip through the slit and glue the ends of the strip together to form a link. Have children continue attaching strips to make a chain. Help children connect the last link through a slit on the second black circle.

In Every Classroom

C

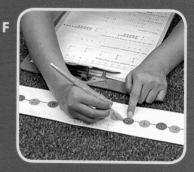

F

D

A

G

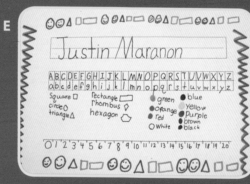

E

B

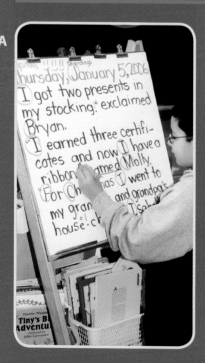

A

C

B

D

Daily Morning Routines

Anchor Charts

C

D

E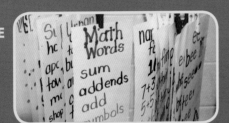

F

G

B

A

C

B

H

G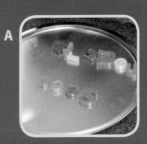

D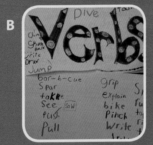

E

F

I

A

Language Arts and Comprehension Strategies

Hands-on Math

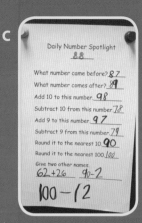

C

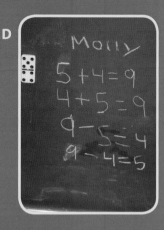

D

I

B

F

L

M

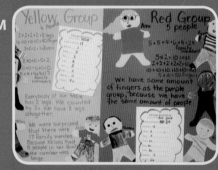

E

A

H

G

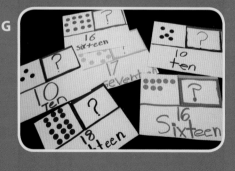

N

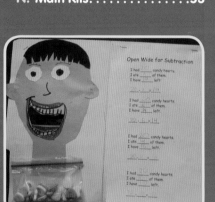

J

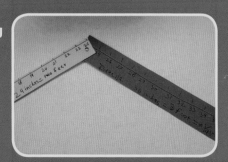

K

Bulletin Boards and Displays with Curricular Connections

D

B

E

F

C

A

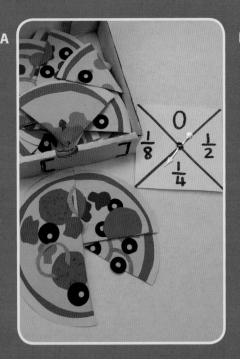

A

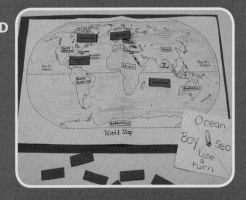

D

C

B

Learning Games

Materials

◄ chart paper
◄ Suggested book:
  In Enzo's Splendid Garden by Patricia Polacco (Philomel)
◄ 12" x 18" (30.5 x 46 cm) construction paper in assorted colors
◄ 12" x 18" (30.5 x 46 cm) question mark-shaped card stock tracers
◄ markers

Questions, Anyone?

Questioning is an important comprehension strategy that can lead to better understanding. Help children learn about different types of comprehension-boosting questioning by inviting them to lead their own literature discussion as they ask and answer questions about a story the class has read. Use this activity with any book related to the reading curriculum or topic being studied.

Children will . . .

• Ask questions to better understand a story
• Lead their own discussion of a story
• Model for one another different types of questions that can be asked

Procedure

1) Write *Before Reading, During Reading,* and *After Reading* as headings across the top of a sheet of chart paper.

2) Show the cover of the book and record any questions children have under the *Before Reading* heading. As you read aloud the story, record any questions that arise under the *During Reading* heading. After the story is finished, record children's questions under the *After Reading* heading.

3) Have children trace the question mark onto construction paper and cut it out. Invite children to write one question about the story (or from the chart) they do not know the answer to on the question mark.

4) Direct children to sit in a circle with their question marks in front of them. Invite children to take turns asking their questions. Allow discussion to continue until all questions are answered. Then ask children to return to their seats and write the answers to their questions on the back of their question marks.

Nonfiction Facts

Nonfiction books are rich with facts! These facts can be found in features such as captions, illustrations, fact boxes, and bold text. Teaching children to search these features to find facts is essential to their comprehension of nonfiction text. Tailor this activity to any topic of study or curricular concept.

Children will . . .

- Learn about different nonfiction features
- Identify facts from a nonfiction book
- Complete a graphic organizer
- Use comprehension strategies when reading

Standards Check

- ◄ Understand and interpret a variety of literary texts
- ◄ Use the general skills and strategies of the reading process
- ◄ Use grammatical and mechanical conventions in written work

Materials

- ◄ Nonfiction Facts reproducible (page 67)
- ◄ 4' x 4' (1.2 x 1.2 m) piece of butcher paper
- ◄ colored art tape
- ◄ Suggested book: *How Earthworms Grow* (The Wright Group)
- ◄ markers

Procedure

1) Create a large graphic organizer by dividing butcher paper into columns, one for each feature you would like to focus on (for example, *Captions, Illustrations, Fact Boxes*, and *Bold Text*). Use colored tape to divide sections.

2) Read aloud *How Earthworms Grow* and have children share facts they learned. Record these facts on the graphic organizer. Ask children to identify the nonfiction feature where they found the facts, and place a check mark under each appropriate column.

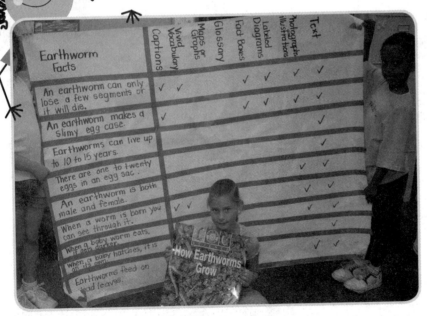

3) Have children work in pairs to complete their own graphic organizer (page 67) using the chart as a resource.

Materials

◄ Suggested book:
  My Father's Dragon
  by Ruth Stiles Gannett (Random House)
◄ white construction paper
◄ markers
◄ book rings

A Picture in Your Mind

Visualizing images when listening to a story can increase children's understanding and comprehension. Capitalize on children's innate ability to use their five senses to visualize a story. Create a class big book of the images children visualize while hearing a story. Use any story with strong descriptive language.

Children will . . .

• Use visualizing as a comprehension strategy
• Illustrate scenes from a story
• Write captions to accompany illustrations

Procedure

1) Read the story aloud to the class over a three-day period. Do not show the illustrations to the children. Wrap the cover with paper so that no clues are given away. If children are not already familiar with the term "visualize," introduce the new vocabulary. Ask the children to close their eyes and "visualize" the story as you read.

2) After the story is completed, have each child illustrate a scene from the story on white construction paper. Ask children to write captions to explain their scenes.

3) Have children order the illustrations sequentially. Laminate the pages and bind them into a book. Discuss the class-created book and how visualizing led to understanding the story. For a fun extension, compare children's illustrations with the artist's illustrations.

4) Place the book in your reading center as an example of how visualizing can aid comprehension.

Synthesizing Puzzles

Learning to synthesize information is a difficult yet important comprehension strategy. Help young children learn to synthesize information from a story by assembling individual story pieces into a complete puzzle. Use any book with simple, clear story elements.

Children will . . .

- Identify individual story elements and characteristics
- Use comprehension strategies when reading
- Assemble a class puzzle to synthesize a story

Standards Check

- ◄ Use the general skills and strategies of the reading process
- ◄ Understand and interpret a variety of literary texts

Materials

- ◄ Suggested book: *The Very Hungry Caterpillar* by Eric Carle (Philomel)
- ◄ chart paper
- ◄ markers
- ◄ white poster board
- ◄ large blank floor puzzle

Procedure

1) Read *The Very Hungry Caterpillar* to the class. As a group, discuss the story elements—title, characters, setting, and story events. Record these on a chart labeled *Story Elements*.

2) In advance, create a puzzle from white poster board or purchase a premade puzzle. Ask each child to look at the chart and choose one element of the book to draw on a blank puzzle piece. Have children include words on each piece that tell what they drew.

3) Place all the pieces on the floor, and as a group, put the puzzle together.

4) Discuss how all the pieces together make the puzzle complete and also make the book complete. Explain that each part is important to understanding the whole story. Place the puzzle pieces in a resealable plastic bag to be kept at the reading center.

Standards Check

◄ Use the general skills and strategies of the reading process
◄ Understand and interpret a variety of literary texts
◄ Use grammatical and mechanical conventions in written work

Materials

◄ 5 ½" x 4 ½" (13.97 x 11.43 cm) mini file folders
◄ 4" x 6" (10 x 15 cm) index cards
◄ markers

Strategies Minifolder

Learning various comprehension strategies is essential to understanding text. Creating this handy reference guide will aid children in understanding and using sophisticated strategies such as synthesizing and inferring. These minifolders are sure to intrigue and motivate children to apply these strategies when reading.

Children will . . .

• Learn definitions and terminology of various comprehension strategies
• Create comprehension strategies folders to use as reference tools
• Use comprehension strategies when reading

Procedure

1) Purchase mini file folders from a teacher supply store. Give each child a minifolder with six index cards. Have children label the folder *Strategies That Work Ideas.*

2) Choose one of the following comprehension strategies to focus on: *Making Connections, Questioning, Nonfiction Features, Visualizing, Inferring,* or *Synthesizing.* Use a think-aloud to model how the particular strategy can help you understand a story, and create a definition as a class.

3) Ask children to write the comprehension strategy on the front side of an index card and the definition on the back. Invite children to decorate the front of the card.

4) Continue this process for each comprehension strategy as it is learned. Encourage children to keep these minifolders handy during reading workshop and when responding to literature.

Classroom Book Nook

Children often limit themselves to one genre or favorite author they enjoy. Expose your students to a variety of genres and authors by creating a Classroom Book Nook together. Children will be sure to read a greater variety of books after they have created the categories for the classroom library and helped organize it.

Children will . . .
• Sort and classify books
• Read a variety of books

Standards Check

◄ Understand and interpret a variety of literary texts
◄ Use the general skills and strategies of the reading process

Materials

◄ chart paper
◄ classroom library collection
◄ 5" x 7" (13 x 18 cm) index cards
◄ markers
◄ baskets or boxes

Procedure

1) Show the children the classroom library. Ask them how they think the class should organize the books. Record their responses on chart paper. Categories may include fiction, nonfiction, poetry, authors, and chapter books.

2) Decide as a class which categories will be used. Record these on a chart labeled *Book Categories*.

3) Place children into small groups. Give each group a stack of books and a number of index cards equal to the number of different categories chosen. Have each group write a category name on each card and lay the cards out on the floor. Then invite children to browse through the books and place them beside the corresponding category card.

4) Label the book baskets or boxes with the chosen category names. Have each group place its sorted piles into the correct baskets or boxes. Invite children to read a book from a new genre or author.

Hands-on Math

Interactive Lessons That Use Manipulatives to Strengthen Understanding

Mystery Addend Cards

Contents

Bugs on Leaves

The concept of addition becomes fun and concrete when spiders are used as counters! Enhance children's understanding of the various addition combinations of 10 using plastic versions of these creepy crawly creatures. The final products make an excellent display for a bulletin board.

Children will . . .

- Use concrete objects to represent number combinations
- Identify number combinations that make 10
- Write addition number sentences
- Create and solve math problems involving one-step addition

Procedure

1) Model number combinations using eight large plastic spiders on large leaf cutouts. As you use the spiders to model various number combinations, record the matching number sentences on a chart labeled *Addition Combinations for 8*.

2) Have each child choose 2 leaf cutouts and 10 confetti spiders.

3) Ask children to glue their 2 leaves to black construction paper. Have children divide their confetti spiders onto the 2 leaves to create an addition problem and glue them in place.

4) Have children write the corresponding addition number sentence on a blank address label and attach it to the black background. Let children write their name on a second address label and attach it.

5) As a group, record all the number combinations that made 10 on a chart labeled *Addition Combinations for 10*.

Standards Check

◄ Use basic and advanced properties of number concepts
◄ Use basic and advanced procedures to perform computation
◄ Use a variety of strategies in the problem-solving process

Materials

◄ Open Wide for Subtraction reproducible (page 68)
◄ legal-sized file folders
◄ stapler
◄ construction paper
◄ scissors, markers, glue
◄ sandwich and snack-sized resealable plastic bags
◄ tape
◄ wrapped candies

Open Wide for Subtraction

Using concrete objects to represent number combinations helps strengthen children's understanding of more symbolic concepts such as number sentences. Children will love "eating" their way to understanding subtraction!

Children will . . .

• Use concrete objects to model the process of subtraction
• Write subtraction number sentences

Procedure

1) In advance, prepare a file folder for each child. Open the file folders and staple a recording sheet to the right side of each folder. Give children construction paper, scissors, markers, and glue to use in making pictures of their face and hair. Invite children to add open mouths and other facial features. Ask children to glue their completed face on the top left side of the file folder opposite the recording sheet.

2) Help children cut a hole through the open mouth and folder. Have children tape a sandwich bag behind the hole on the back of the folder. Then have children tape a snack-sized resealable bag below the front of the face. Give children 10 candies to place in the snack bag. Adjust the number of candies to meet individual needs.

3) Have children act out the subtraction process by placing some of the candies into the open mouth of the face on their folder. Ask children to record a number sentence for each subtraction problem they act out.

Daily Number Spotlight

This chart activity is a great way to reinforce a variety of mathematical concepts each day. Use it as a warm-up to math time, or create a mini-version of your chart to place at the math center for individual practice.

Children will . . .

- Use beginning mathematical concepts such as rounding, number order, and place value
- Determine questions to ask about numbers
- Use flexible thinking strategies

Standards Check

- Use basic and advanced properties of number concepts
- Use a variety of strategies in the problem-solving process

Materials

- chart paper
- markers
- overhead markers

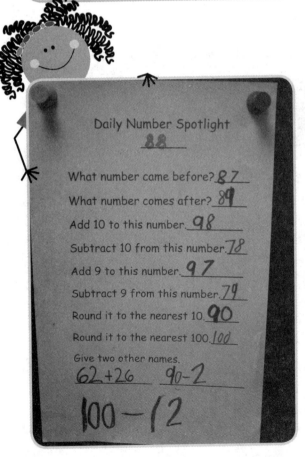

Procedure

1) Choose a number to spotlight. This can be the number matching the number of days in school or any other number the class is working with in math.

2) Label a sheet of chart paper *Daily Number Spotlight*. Below the heading draw a box in which the special number can be written.

3) Record on the chart 10 questions children have about the number. Possible questions include *What number comes before it?*, *What number comes after it?*, *What number is 10 more?*, and *What is the number rounded to the nearest 10?*

4) Laminate the chart, and use an overhead marker to easily change the number being spotlighted and the answers to the questions each day. Invite children to choose the number, read the questions, and record the answers.

5) Periodically change the questions, and make a new chart to keep the interest fresh and support the concepts your class is learning.

Materials

◄ Domino Fact Families reproducible (page 69)

◄ dominoes (regular and oversized)

◄ chart paper

◄ self-adhesive magnets

◄ coffee can

Fact Family Magnets

Fact families help children understand the relationship between addition and subtraction, and strengthen their number sense. Using dominoes to make fact family magnets is a fun and easy way to reinforce the concept.

Children will . . .

• Identify members of a fact family

• Record number sentences to represent fact families

• Understand and use the inverse relationship between addition and subtraction

Procedure

1) Model the concept of fact families using the oversized dominoes. For example, a domino with 2 dots on the left side and 3 dots on the right side creates a fact family for the number 5 (e.g., 2+3, 3+2, 5-3, and 5-2). Record number sentences on a chart labeled *Fact Families*.

2) Have children choose a variety of the small dominoes and record the fact families they discover on the *Domino Fact Families* recording sheet.

3) Invite children to make a fact family magnet by attaching a self-adhesive magnet to the back of a domino. Ask children to take home their magnet and place it on the refrigerator.

Optional: To reinforce the concept, have children make additional magnets to attach on the outside of a large coffee can or filing cabinet. Reproduce copies of page 69, and place them with the magnets at a math center. Encourage children to choose magnets from the can and record the fact families they discover.

Magic In and Out Box

Using mathematical reasoning and number sense to discover patterns enables children to be creative problem solvers. After observing several examples, children can be the experts and become the rule makers for this fun activity. Place this "magic box" at the math center for pairs and small groups to use.

Children will . . .
- Identify patterns in numbers
- Solve problems with unknown operations

Procedure

1) Cover the outside bottom and sides of a box with butcher paper. Lay the box on its side so that the bottom becomes the front of your "magic box." Use construction paper to decorate the box with brightly colored numbers. Cut two holes in the front of the box large enough for an adult hand to fit through. Label these holes *in* and *out*. Use colored art tape to create smooth edges around the holes and along the borders of the box.

2) Draw a line dividing the 12" x 18" (30.5 x 46 cm) piece of construction paper in half vertically. Label one side *in*, and label the other side *out*. Attach sticky notes under the *in* heading and lay the chart in front of the box. Have a set of sticky notes available behind the box as well. Have children record each number that goes in and comes out on the chart.

3) Think of a simple operation (e.g., *add 2*), but do not tell the class. Have a child write a number on a sticky note and place it through the *in* hole. Take this number and apply the secret operation (e.g., *add 2*). Write the answer on a sticky note and send this back through the *out* hole. When children think they know the secret operation, have them predict the outcome of the next number. If they answer correctly, ask them to tell the rule of the "magic box."

Standards Check

- Use basic and advanced properties of number concepts
- Use basic and advanced procedures to perform computation
- Use a variety of strategies in the problem-solving process

Materials

- construction paper in fall colors
- scissors
- glue
- 9" x 12" (23 x 30.5 cm) black construction paper
- blank address labels
- markers

Leaf Arrays

Learning to create an array strengthens children's understanding of the relationship between repeated addition and multiplication. Autumn is a perfect time to make arrays using the colors of fall leaves. Children will delight in arranging colorful leaves in equal rows to create their own stunning arrays. The group's efforts make a wonderful autumn bulletin board.

Children will . . .

- Use arrays, repeated addition, and counting multiples to perform multiplication
- Demonstrate the meaning of addition and multiplication
- Write addition and multiplication number sentences

Procedure

1) Model the concept of arrays and their connection to repeated addition and multiplication.

2) Have children cut out autumn-colored leaf shapes to use in their arrays or provide them with pre-cut leaf shapes for this purpose.

3) Invite children to glue an equal number of leaves in separate rows on the black construction paper to create an array. Encourage children to make each row in their array a different color to strengthen the visual representation.

4) Ask children to write a matching addition or multiplication number sentence on a blank address label and attach it beside the array. Have children use a second address label to write and attach their name to their paper.

Mystery Addend Cards

Finding the missing addend strengthens children's understanding of number relationships and builds a foundation for algebra concepts. To make this concept concrete, have children make their own missing addend riddle cards. Use these cards in a group activity or keep them in the math center for individual practice.

Children will . . .

• Solve addition and subtraction problems involving missing addends
• Understand the inverse relationship between addition and subtraction

Standards Check

◄ Use basic and advanced properties of number concepts
◄ Use basic and advanced procedures to perform computation
◄ Use a variety of strategies in the problem-solving process

Materials

◄ sample cards (see Step 2 under "Procedure")
◄ 8" x 10" (20 x 25.5 cm) white construction paper
◄ markers
◄ dot stickers
◄ 4" x 5" (10 x 13 cm) white construction paper
◄ colored art tape

Procedure

1) Show the children a sample card and ask, *How many dots are hiding under the question mark?* Discuss the part/part/whole card.

2) Model for children how to make their own card. First, fold the large piece of construction paper in half lengthwise, and use a marker to draw a line over the fold. Write the chosen number as a numeral and number word below the line. Draw a second line to divide the top portion of the paper into two equal squares.

3) Take the corresponding number of dot stickers and place some in the left square and the remainder in the right square. Draw a question mark on the small piece of construction paper, and use colored art tape to attach it to the upper right hand corner of the large piece of paper to make a flap. Have children choose a number and make their own card.

4) Invite children to sit in a circle and one at a time hold up their cards. Ask children to choose a classmate to solve the problem. Continue until all have shared their cards.

Materials

◄ chart paper
◄ hundreds charts
◄ stapler
◄ glue
◄ markers

Secret Numbers

What's more fun than knowing a secret number and waiting for others to guess? In this activity, children use their knowledge of more and less and place value to narrow the field and discover the secret number.

Children will . . .

• Use knowledge of more and less to solve a problem
• Practice number sense skills
• Understand and use numbers up to 100

Procedure

1) Cut chart paper into thirds and give each child a piece. Have children fold the paper in thirds to create a folder. Staple five copies of a hundreds chart to the right inside page of their folders. Ask children to glue an additional hundreds chart to the back of the folder. Instruct children to write the words *Secret Numbers* on the cover of the folder and decorate it.

2) Ask children to circle a secret number between 1 and 100 on the hundreds chart glued to the back of their folder. Invite children to try and guess other students' secret numbers by taking turns asking questions such as, "Is your number less than 10?" Have one child at a time ask the questions until they guess the number.

3) Encourage children to use the hundreds chart to help them ask and answer questions. For example, if a child asks, "Is the number between 10 and 20?" and the answer is no, then that child can cross off numbers 11–19 on the hundreds chart inside his or her folder.

4) Help children to understand how the field of numbers narrows as the guesses are made. Invite children to take these folders home and practice the skill with their family.

Clockworks

Learning to read and understand an analog clock is difficult for many children. Telling time will have greater meaning when children can manipulate the hands on the clocks as they practice identifying times. Learning to tell time will be fun and easy with these Clockworks books!

Children will . . .

- Set clock hands to given times
- Tell time to the hour and half hour
- Write word problems involving time
- Solve word problems with elapsed time

Standards Check

- ◄ Use basic and advanced properties of measurement concepts
- ◄ Use a variety of strategies in the problem-solving process

Materials

- ◄ 5" x 12" (13 x 30.5 cm) construction paper
- ◄ clock stamp—at least 3" (7.5 cm) in diameter
- ◄ utility knife
- ◄ spiral bookbinding
- ◄ large and small paper clips
- ◄ brass fasteners

The class went to the zoo at 10:30 am. They came back at 2:15. How long was the trip to the zoo?

Avneet

Procedure

1) Prepare a Clockworks book for each child. Stamp the back page with a clock face and laminate. Cut a small slit in the center of the clock for children to insert a brass fastener and attach the hands of the clock. Create six inside pages with an open circle cutout allowing the clock face on the back page to show through. Use a utility knife to cut through multiple layers of paper at a time. Add a cover titled *Clockworks,* and bind the pages together at the top to make a flipbook.

2) Ask children to draw a clock face on the cover. Assist children in adding large and small paperclip "hands" to the clock on the back page with the brass fastener.

3) Have children write a sentence on each page, such as *I wake up at 7:00 a.m.* or *We have recess at 10:00 a.m.* Encourage children who are ready to write a word problem on each page, such as *I eat lunch at 12:00 p.m. I eat for 30 minutes. What time will I be finished?*

4) Invite children to set the "hands" of their practice clock to show the times for each sentence or word problem.

Standards Check

◄ Use basic and advanced properties of measurement concepts
◄ Use a variety of strategies in the problem-solving process

Materials

◄ Folding Yardsticks Recording Sheet reproducible (page 70)
◄ 1 ½" x 13" strips of yellow poster board
◄ 1 ½" x 14" strips of red and blue poster board
◄ rulers
◄ thin-tipped black markers
◄ hole punches
◄ brass fasteners

Folding Yardsticks

Measuring is fun with these handmade folding yardsticks! When children create their own measuring tools, the concept of and relationship between inches, feet, and yards becomes concrete. As an added bonus, the folding yardsticks can be stored easily inside desks!

Children will . . .

• Convert 12 inches into one foot and 3 feet into one yard
• Estimate measurements
• Measure objects using inches, feet, and yards
• Use standard measurement tools

Procedure

1) Give each child a yellow strip. Have children use a ruler to mark the strip in inch increments and number these marks from 1 to 12.

2) Give each child a red strip. Have children use a ruler to mark the strip in inch increments and number these marks from 12 to 24.

3) Give each child a blue strip. Have children use a ruler to mark the strip in inch increments and number these marks from 24 to 36.

4) Ask children to hole-punch below the 12 on the yellow and red strips, place them on top of one another, and connect them with a brass fastener. Ask children to hole-punch below the 24 on the red and blue strips, place them on top of one another, and connect them with a brass fastener.

5) Invite children to estimate lengths of objects around the classroom and then measure them with the folding yardsticks. Have children record estimates and actual measurements on the Folding Yardsticks Recording Sheet.

Decorated Tree Combinations

Finding all possible combinations of outcomes helps children become flexible thinkers. Children choose a tree shape and different decorations to create various combinations. They will love to predict the number of possible outcomes.

Children will . . .
- Estimate combination outcomes
- Sort and classify objects according to one or more attributes
- Organize information on a graph or grid to solve a problem

Standards Check
◄ Recognize regularities in designs, shapes, and sets of numbers/extend simple patterns
◄ Collect and represent information about objects or events in simple graphs
◄ Use a variety of strategies in the problem-solving process

Materials
◄ chart paper
◄ butcher paper
◄ fir tree, holly tree, and pine tree card stock tracers
◄ green construction paper
◄ scissors
◄ buttons
◄ tissue paper
◄ snowflake confetti
◄ glue

Procedure

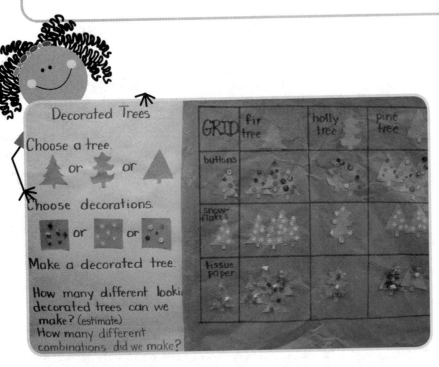

1) Write activity directions on chart paper labeled *Decorated Trees*, and read them to the class. On butcher paper, create a 3' x 3' (0.9 x 0.9 m) grid with the tree choice names and pictures along the top and the decoration choices listed along the side.

2) Have children predict how many differently decorated trees can be made. Record their estimations.

3) Ask children to choose one type of tree and one decoration to make a decorated tree. Have children attach their trees to the grid as they are made. Be sure all combinations are represented.

4) Discuss the information on the grid. Have children identify how many different combinations of decorated trees were made. For those children who are ready, introduce multiplication to solve combination word problems.

Materials

◄ 7' x 7' (2.13 x 2.13 m) brown butcher paper
◄ markers
◄ construction paper
◄ glue
◄ scissors
◄ tape
◄ 3" x 5" (7.5 x 13 cm) index cards
◄ gardening area (optional)
◄ string (optional)

Garden Plot

Arranging and describing objects in space strengthens geometric knowledge. Plan a garden with the children using a coordinate grid. Flowers made by the children will mark specific coordinates on the grid. To make this experience even more special, plant a real garden based on the grid!

Children will . . .

• Identify the x-axis and y-axis on a coordinate grid
• Identify coordinates on a grid
• Find designated points using coordinates

Procedure

1) Draw lines to divide the butcher paper into 12" x 12" (30.5 x 30.5 cm) squares. Label the x-axis and the y-axis with numbers 1 to 7. Explain the grid to the children using the terms *grid* and *coordinates*.

2) Have children make small flowers from construction paper and place them on the garden grid. Ask children to label the coordinates of their flowers on an index card and tape it to the grid. A variation is for the teacher to state the coordinates and then have children place the flowers.

Optional: Plant a real garden marked with string to make a grid. Use the paper grid to guide the planting.

Group Inventories

Creating inventories is a fun and easy way for children to learn about data collection. In this activity, children count items in small groups to complete an inventory. Comparing the results from each group's inventory will allow children to use deductive reasoning skills.

Children will . . .
- Count objects common to a small group of children
- Use concrete, pictorial, and symbolic representations of numbers
- Create repeated addition and multiplication number sentences
- Compare and interpret information from group inventories

Standards Check
◄ Collect and represent information about objects or events in simple graphs
◄ Use basic and advanced properties of numbers concepts
◄ Use basic and advanced procedures to perform computation

Materials
◄ Group Inventory reproducible (page 71)
◄ chart paper
◄ 2' x 3' (61 x 91.4 cm) butcher paper charts
◄ 12" (30.5 cm) child-shaped tracers
◄ construction paper
◄ scissors
◄ markers
◄ glue

Procedure

1) Model data collection by creating a class inventory. Brainstorm with children a list of items found in the classroom, such as clocks, desks, and windows. As a group, record the number of each item on a chart. Explain to children they will work in small groups to create a group inventory.

2) Give each group a Group Inventory recording sheet and a different colored piece of butcher paper. Have children complete the inventory-recording sheet together and glue it to the chart. Facilitate small group discussions to help children use words and number sentences to record their findings.

3) Have children use child-shaped tracers, construction paper, and markers to create self-representations. Ask children to glue these to the butcher paper chart.

4) Bring all groups together to discuss their charts. Ask questions like *Why do 5 children in a group have 10 legs?* and *Will 5 children always have 8 buttons? Why or Why not?* Record their conclusions on chart paper.

Materials

Each child will need the following:
◄ 1 plastic pencil box
◄ 20 two-sided counters
◄ 20 base ten ones cubes
◄ 10 base ten tens rods
◄ 1 base ten hundreds flat
◄ 20 Unifix cubes (10 each of two colors)
◄ 1 six-inch (15 cm) ruler
◄ 2 dice
◄ 1 permanent marker

Math Kits

When young hands manipulate objects, they are more likely to learn and understand math concepts. Make math time easy by having children make individual math kits containing the manipulatives used most often in the primary classroom. These can be easily stored in desks or stacked at the math center, ready to use each day!

Children will . . .

• Count math manipulatives
• Inventory math manipulatives
• Use concrete objects to solve math problems

Procedure

1) Create manipulative stations by placing all of the manipulatives children will need in their kits on tables around the room. Use an index card to label each manipulative with the number of items each child should place in his or her kit (e.g., the number *20* should be taped to the container of two-sided counters). Follow this procedure with all of the manipulatives children will need.

2) Provide each child with a pencil box. Have children use a permanent marker to personalize their kit. For example, *Joe's Math Kit*.

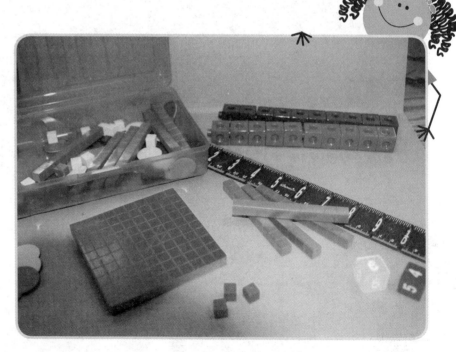

3) Have children move around the room and collect the designated number of each manipulative. These should all fit nicely in the pencil box. Store math kits in desks or at a math center. Encourage children to use the kit when they are working independently or with the class.

Bulletin Boards and Displays
with Curricular Connections

Student-Demonstrated Learning through Integrated Disciplines

Data Retrieval Charts

Contents

Standards Check

◄ Use descriptive words to convey basic ideas
◄ Use grammatical and mechanical conventions in written work

Materials

◄ chart paper
◄ construction paper in assorted colors
◄ scissors
◄ glue
◄ markers
◄ blue poster board
◄ manila paper

Instead of Said

Children love to shout, cheer, and whisper! Integrate writing and art to help them avoid overused words and expand their writing vocabulary. Initially display children's work on a bulletin board, and then assemble the pages into a big book. This big book will be a favorite resource in the writing center!

Children will . . .

• Generate alternative words for *said*
• Expand oral and written vocabulary
• Learn how to punctuate dialogue
• Create a classroom thesaurus

Procedure

1) Label a class chart *Instead of Said*. Keep a running list of alternative words for *said* as you read various books.

2) Have children choose one of the words from the list. Give children construction paper, scissors, and glue and ask them to make their own face and upper torso. Ask children to use markers to make features depicting an expression that matches their chosen word. For example, an open mouth for *exclaimed*, a closed smile for *giggled*, or a frown for *moaned*.

3) Cut poster board in half. Give children one half and ask them to glue the faces on the poster board. Give children manila paper and ask them to write a phrase that matches their expression. For example, *"Don't tickle me!" giggled Hannah*, or *"I won the game!" cheered Nik*. Have children make a speech bubble around the words, cut out the bubble, and glue it to the poster board. To accentuate the punctuation, have children use a red marker to write punctuation marks.

Measuring Sunflowers

This sunny garden display offers opportunities for learning about a variety of measuring tools and comparing units of measure. Children will become comfortable with customary measuring terminology, as they create a garden of sunflowers in their classroom.

Children will . . .

- Use standard and nonstandard measurement tools
- Measure in increments of inches, feet, yards, centimeters, and meters

Standards Check

◄ Understand and apply basic and advanced properties of measurement concepts

Materials

◄ fiction and nonfiction books on sunflowers
◄ green, yellow, brown, and dark brown construction paper
◄ scissors
◄ tape
◄ rulers with inches and centimeters
◄ yardsticks and metersticks
◄ markers
◄ sunflower seeds (optional)

Procedure

1) Provide children with a variety of sunflower books as resources. Invite children to work in pairs and help each other cut strips from 12" x 18" (30.5 x 46 cm) green construction paper. Have children tape their strips together to make one stem as tall as they are.

2) Ask children to use brown and yellow construction paper to create a sunflower. Seeds can be added using dark brown paper or real sunflower seeds. Have children create leaves and tape them to their stem.

3) Instruct children to measure the length of their stem by using their sunflower as a nonstandard unit. Have them record the measurement on the front side of the stem. For example, *8 sunflowers long*. Ask children to measure and record the length of their stem using various standard units of measure (e.g., inches, centimeters, feet, meters). Remind children to label the different units of measure they use. Discuss similarities and differences in units of measure. *Optional:* Invite children to measure the length of their leaves and petals, or ask children to record a number sentence representing the number of seeds in the center of their sunflower.

Interpreting Graphs

Cross-curricular study supports learning in many subject areas. Incorporate math and art into science or social studies while aiding children's ability to construct and interpret graphs. Tailor this activity to any curricular concept.

Children will . . .
- Use gathered data to create a graph
- Interpret information depicted on a graph to create a picture

Standards Check
- Gather and use information for research purposes
- Understand the relationships among organisms and their physical environment
- Collect and represent information about objects or events in simple graphs

Materials
- books about the desert
- chart paper
- graph paper
- construction paper in assorted colors
- scissors
- glue
- thin-tipped black markers

Procedure

1) After reading several desert books to the class, have children discuss desert characteristics. Record their findings on a chart labeled *The Desert*. Have children choose eight to ten favorite items from the list, and circle them.

2) Use tally marks to represent the number of each item (circled in Step 1) you would like children to show on their graph. Have children use the information from the chart to complete their graph. For example, if there are five tally marks beside the desert characteristic *cactus,* then children will color in five boxes above that item on their graph.

3) Model how to use the information from their graphs to create a picture. For example, if there are five cacti represented on the graph, there will be five cacti in the picture. Invite children to use construction paper and cut out objects to glue on their picture. Encourage children to use a thin-tipped black marker to add details.

4) Display the graphs alongside the pictures on a bulletin board to demonstrate a range of learning objectives. Invite children to write about what they have learned about the desert.

Data Retrieval Charts

Teaching children to construct graphic organizers, such as data retrieval charts, helps them sort and classify information. Apply the chart outline to many topics, and use it as a resource when children are writing.

Children will . . .
• Read nonfiction books to gain information
• Gather and organize information on a graphic organizer
• Use information from a chart in their writing

Standards Check
◄ Understand and interpret a variety of informational texts
◄ Gather and use information for research purposes
◄ Use the general skills and strategies of the reading process

Materials
◄ colored art tape
◄ 7'–8' (2.13–2.44 m) butcher paper
◄ markers
◄ nonfiction books

Procedure

1) Use colored tape on the butcher paper to make a grid for an enlarged data retrieval chart. In the top left box, label the topic being studied and list examples down the left side (e.g., topic—plants & fungi, examples—mushroom, cactus, tulip). Decide as a class what categories should be written along the top of the chart. Act as the "guide on the side," leading the children to good choices through discussion (e.g., Where does it grow? What does it need?).

2) Place children into small groups, and provide them with books on the topic. Have groups take notes on the facts they find. Invite parent volunteers to aid in this process.

3) Have the groups come together as a class and share the information they found. Ask children to record their ideas on the large class chart.

4) Encourage children to write a report using the chart as a resource.

◄ Use the general skills and strategies of the reading process

◄ Understand relationships among organisms and their physical environment

◄ Use grammatical and mechanical conventions in written work

Materials

◄ chart paper

◄ nonfiction books about the forest

◄ 9" x 12" (23 x 30.5 cm) manila paper

◄ markers and crayons

◄ 12" x 18" (30.5 x 46 cm) construction paper in assorted colors

◄ glue

◄ sentence strips

Diurnal/Nocturnal Folders

Each environment has creatures and plants that are interdependent and unique. Children will learn which plant life and animals in a habitat are diurnal or nocturnal. Use this activity for any habitat you are studying.

Children will . . .

• Investigate life processes

• Identify diurnal and nocturnal plants and animals

• Classify animals by characteristics

Procedure

1) Introduce the vocabulary terms *diurnal* and *nocturnal*. After you have read several books on forest animals with the class, invite children to review the books in small groups and classify the animals as *diurnal* and *nocturnal*.

2) Give children two pieces of manila paper. Ask them to illustrate a daytime forest scene on one piece that includes five diurnal animals and illustrate the same forest scene at night (with five nocturnal animals) on the second piece. Have children label each animal and color the background of the daytime forest light blue and the nighttime forest black.

3) Help children fold the two ends of a piece of construction paper to create a display folder. Ask children to glue the nocturnal scene inside. Show children how to fold their diurnal scenes in half vertically, cut on the fold, and glue each half on the outside flaps of their folder.

4) Invite children to write facts about diurnal and nocturnal forest animals on the inside flaps. Help children create and attach sentence strip labels to the top of their illustrations. Display the folders in a science center.

Pollinating Bees

Understanding scientific concepts is enhanced when children participate in hands-on experiences. Children will learn about the concept of pollination as their child-made bees fly from flower to flower in your classroom!

Children will . . .
- Make a model of a bee
- Simulate the act of pollination
- Understand how pollination works
- Describe their observations

Standards Check
- Understand relationships among organisms and their physical environment
- Understand the nature of scientific inquiry
- Use grammatical and mechanical conventions in written work

Materials
- books about pollination
- 6" (15 cm) white tagboard ovals
- black and yellow markers
- scissors and staplers
- white tulle (netting)
- yellow pipe cleaners
- cotton swabs
- real mums or daffodils
- magnifying glasses

Procedure

1) Read aloud a variety of books about pollination as background information for this activity.

2) To make bee models, have children color two paper ovals on one side with black and yellow markers. Invite children to cut wings out of tulle. Have children bend a yellow pipe cleaner in half for antennae. For demonstration purposes, children will only need one cotton swab to represent the bee's hind legs and simulate the act of pollination. Assist children in stapling the two ovals, wings, antennae, and cotton swab together.

3) Have children simulate the act of pollination using their bee models and the mums. Invite children to collect pollen from the mum on the bee's back leg (cotton swab). Ask children to use magnifying glasses to observe the pollen collected on the cotton swab (bee's leg).

4) Have children draw and describe in writing the act of pollination in their science journals. Mount bees on wooden dowels and insert into potted plants. Display the bees and flowers with children's recorded observations in the science center.

Learning Games

Games to Reinforce Curricular-Based Skills

A Slice of Pizza

Contents

A Slice of Pizza

Children are exposed to the concept of fractions everyday without even realizing it. Enhance their understandings of fractions, conceptually and symbolically, and make learning fun by having them create their own pizza games. The children's tummies might growl when they play this one!

Children will . . .

- Identify whole, ½, ¼, and ⅛.
- Identify fractional parts of a set and write the corresponding fractions
- Create an interactive fractions game

Standards Check

- ◄ Use a variety of strategies in the problem-solving process
- ◄ Use basic and advanced properties of number concepts

Materials

- ◄ A Slice of Pizza directions reproducible (page 72)
- ◄ Blank Spinners reproducible (page 80)
- ◄ 8" (20 cm) manila, 7" (18 cm) red, and 6" (15 cm) yellow construction paper circles
- ◄ construction paper in assorted colors
- ◄ glue, scissors, and markers
- ◄ 4" x 4" (10 x 10 cm) card stock squares
- ◄ paper clips
- ◄ brass fasteners
- ◄ pizza boxes

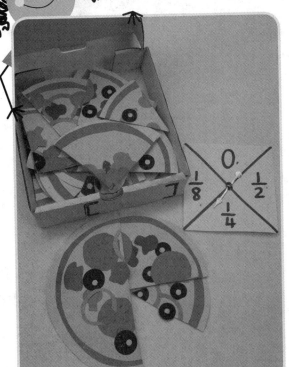

Procedure

1) Have children make three "pizzas." To make pizzas, have children glue the yellow circle on top of the red circle and the red circle on top of the manila circle. Invite children to use construction paper to create different toppings. Encourage using thin layers of glue so that folding and cutting will be easier. Allow these to dry overnight.

2) Ask children to create pizza slices. Have children carefully fold the first pizza in half and cut along the fold to make two halves. Have children fold the second pizza in half and then in half the other direction and cut along the folds to make quarters. Have children fold the third pizza the same as the second pizza to make quarters. Then ask children to fold each of the quarters in half and cut along the folds to make eighths.

3) Instruct children to follow the directions on the reproducible on page 80 to create a spinner. Have children label the four sections *0, ½ , ¼,* and *⅛.* Ask children to place the pizza slices, spinner, and directions card into a pizza box. Review the directions with the class before children play.

Standards Check

◄ Understand relationships among organisms and their physical environment

Materials

◄ What's the Buzzz? game board reproducible (page 74)

◄ What's the Buzzz? directions reproducible (page 72)

◄ What's the Buzzz? Game Cards and answer key reproducibles (page 75–77)

◄ 9" x 12" (23 x 30.5 cm) tagboard pieces

◄ markers

◄ glue

◄ two-sided counters (red/yellow)

◄ scissors

◄ resealable plastic bags

What's the Buzzz?

Games are a fun way to learn or reinforce science concepts and facts. Use this game during or after a thematic unit on insects to reinforce or review facts being learned. Learning about insects is enjoyable when children make and play their own "What's the Buzzz?" game!

Children will . . .

• Learn and review insect facts
• Create an interactive insect game

Procedure

1) Invite children to color the game board and glue it to a tagboard background. Give each child nine two-sided counters. Have children turn five of the counters into ladybug "dice" by adding spots to the red sides with a black permanent marker. Ask children to turn the remaining four counters into ladybug game pieces by adding dots to the yellow side. Remind children to use a different number of dots on each game piece so players know which ladybug belongs to them.

2) Provide children with copies of the question cards and answer key. To make game cards, have children cut apart the question and answer cards and glue the correct answers to the back of the question cards.

3) Have children place the game board, game cards, directions card, ladybug dice, and game pieces in a resealable bag. Review the directions with the class before children play.

The Cinderella Game

Help children enhance their creative thinking and literary skills as they tell their own funny versions of "Cinderella." This game reviews the important elements found in fairy tales and offers opportunities for children to practice oral communication skills.

Children will . . .

- Recognize and understand elements commonly found in fairy tales
- Create a funny "Cinderella" story
- Write new versions of "Cinderella"

Standards Check

- ◄ Understand and interpret a variety of literary texts
- ◄ Use listening and speaking strategies for different purposes

Materials

- ◄ The Cinderella Game game board reproducible (page 78)
- ◄ The Cinderella Game directions reproducible (page 73)
- ◄ 1½" x 3" (4 x 7.5 cm) blank card stock game cards
- ◄ markers or colored pencils
- ◄ two-sided counters
- ◄ mini plastic shoe game tokens
- ◄ resealable plastic bags

Procedure

1) Give each child a game board enlarged onto 11" x 17" (28 x 43 cm) paper, a set of 36 blank game cards, and a directions card. Invite children to color their game boards.

2) Have children create a set of 36 game cards. Ask them to label one side of the cards with one of the following category names (make six of each) *setting*, *hero*, *villain*, *shoe*, *magic*, and *party*. Then, on the reverse side, have children write an appropriate example for each category (e.g., *slipper* or *hiking boot* for "shoe," *wand* or *potion* for "magic," *birthday party* or *Halloween party* for "party"). Encourage children to use examples from fairy tales they have read or make up their own ideas.

3) Give each child four two-sided counters and four plastic shoe game tokens. Ask children to place their game board, directions card, and all game pieces in a resealable bag. Review the directions with the class before children play.

Optional: Have children use their story elements from the game to write a story to share with the class.

Water World

Learning geography and mapping concepts is fun when children play their own Water World game! After playing the game, children will find it easier to explain the difference between oceans, seas, and bays and they will be able to locate these on a world map.

Children will . . .

• Learn geographical terms and definitions for *oceans*, *seas*, and *bays*

• Learn to use a map or globe

• Locate bodies of water on a world map

Procedure

1) Give each child a game board enlarged onto 11" x 17" (28 x 43 cm) paper and a directions card. Have children color their game boards with colored pencils.

2) Create a game card grid template. To make a template, draw a vertical line dividing the copy paper rectangle in half. Then draw five horizontal lines to create twelve equal boxes. Label each box with one of the following: *Arctic Ocean, Chesapeake Bay, Pacific Ocean, Black Sea, Caribbean Sea, Hudson Bay, Atlantic Ocean, North Sea, Mediterranean Sea, Bay of Bengal, Indian Ocean*, and *Red Sea*. Make enough copies for each child. Ask children to carefully cut along the lines to make bodies of water game cards.

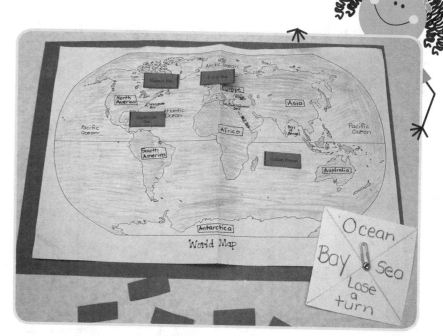

3) Ask children to create a spinner by following the directions on the reproducible on page 80. Have children label the four sections: *ocean, sea, bay*, and *lose a turn*.

4) Have children place all components for the game in a resealable bag. Review the directions with the class before children play.

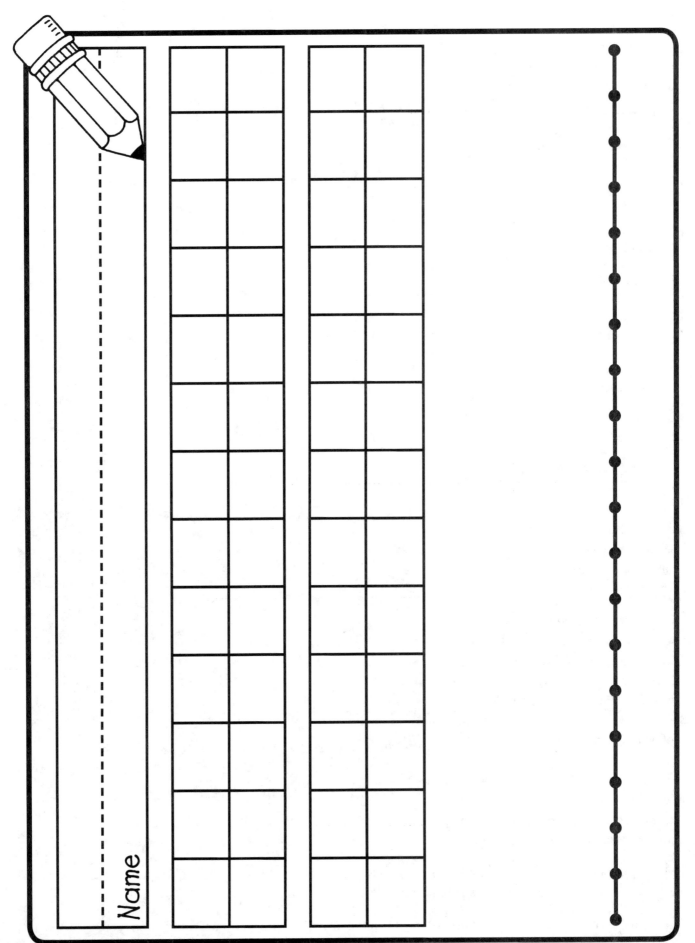

Name

Interactive Projects & Displays © 2006 Creative Teaching Press

Nonfiction Facts

Facts from _____

Record facts in the space below. Where did you find the facts? Put a check mark in the box.

FACTS	Captions	Illustrations	Fact Boxes	Bold Text

Open Wide for Subtraction

I had _____ pieces of candy.
I ate _____ of them.
I have _____ left.

_____ - _____ = _____

I had _____ pieces of candy.
I ate _____ of them.
I have _____ left.

_____ - _____ = _____

I had _____ pieces of candy.
I ate _____ of them.
I have _____ left.

_____ - _____ = _____

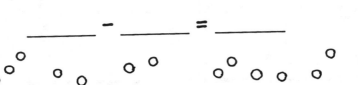

Interactive Projects & Displays © 2006 Creative Teaching Press

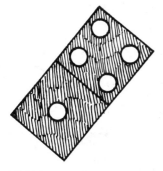

Domino Fact Families

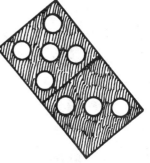

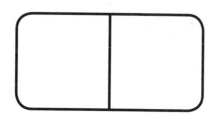

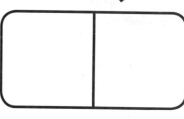

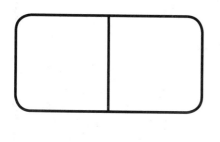

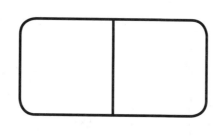

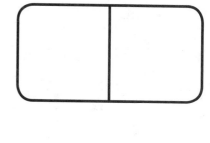

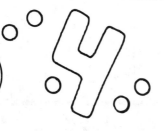
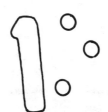

Folding Yardsticks
Recording Sheet

What I Measured	My Estimate	My Measurement	What I Measured With

Group Inventory

Record the number of items for each member in your group.

Group Members_____

Number of family members _____

Number of brothers _____

Number of sisters _____

Number of pets _____

Number of eyes _____

Number of fingers _____

Number of buttons on clothes _____

A Slice of Pizza

For 2-4 players ages 6 & up

Game Directions

1 Each player uses his or her own pizza game box. Keep all pizza slices in the box until needed.

2 The first player spins and takes a slice of pizza from his or her box that is the same size shown on the spinner. Then the next player takes a turn.

3 If the spinner lands on a fraction larger than the player needs, then he or she loses a turn.

4 The winner is the first person to make a whole pizza.

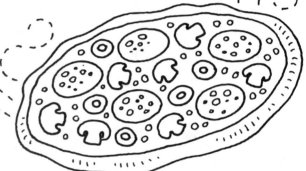

What's the Buzzz?

For 2–4 players ages 6 & up

Game Directions

1 Shuffle the game cards. Lay them question-side up next to the game board.

2 The first player picks up a card and answers the insect question.

3 If the player is correct, he or she tosses the ladybug dice and moves the same number of spaces as the ladybugs that are red side up.
If the player is incorrect, then he or she loses a turn.

4 The winner is the first player to reach the top of the insect jar!

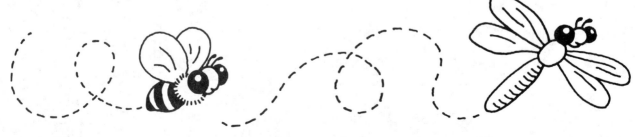

Interactive Projects & Displays © 2006 Creative Teaching Press

The Cinderella Game

For 2-4 players ages 6 & up

Game Directions

1 Sort game cards into six groups by categories. Place game cards along the edge of the game board with the story elements facing up.

2 The first player tosses the four two-sided counters and moves his or her shoe the same number of spaces as the number of red sides showing.

3 The player picks a card matching the space he or she landed on and places it in front of him or her with the story element face up. A player misses a turn if he or she already has the story element.

4 The first player to collect all six story elements wins the game and gets to share his or her funny "Cinderella" story.

Interactive Projects & Displays © 2006 Creative Teaching Press

---

Water World

For 2 players ages 6 & up

Game Directions

1 Shuffle game cards. Divide game cards equally between players.

2 Each player lays game cards face up in front of him or her.

3 The first player spins the spinner and chooses the matching body of water card. The player then places the card on the map in the correct place. If the player does not have a matching card (or if the spinner stops on *lose a turn*), he or she loses a turn.

4 The winner is the first player to run out of cards.

Interactive Projects & Displays © 2006 Creative Teaching Press

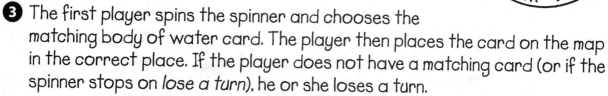

What's the Buzzz?
An Insect Information Game

FINISH

START

What's the Buzzz?
Game Cards

What are the three main body parts of an insect?	Why do honeybees dance?	Where does a praying mantis lay its eggs?
Where are the ears on crickets?	How does a moth protect itself?	Does a butterfly have symmetry?
Are lightning bugs diurnal or nocturnal?	Do all insects lay eggs?	What do ladybugs eat the most?
What is the life cycle of a ladybug?	Are crickets diurnal or nocturnal?	Who is in charge of an ant colony?
What do ants eat?	How does a cricket chirp?	How does a butterfly get nectar?

What's the Buzzz?
Game Cards

What does a praying mantis eat?	Why do lightning bugs glow?	What do honeybees make to cover the honey?
What is the life cycle of a butterfly?	Who is the largest bee in a beehive?	Where do ants live?
How many legs does an insect have?	What is a baby cricket called?	What do butterflies eat?
Does a bee have symmetry?	Where do monarch butterflies go in winter?	Are most moths diurnal or nocturnal?
What moth is known for its green-yellow color?	How do ladybugs protect themselves?	What is another name for a praying mantis?

Interactive Projects & Displays © 2006 Creative Teaching Press

What's the Buzzz?
Answer Key

Answers for game cards on page 75.

head, thorax, abdomen	to communicate	egg case or egg sac	on their knees	camouflage and wing coloration
yes	nocturnal	yes	aphids	egg, larva, pupa, adult
nocturnal	worker ants	seeds, sweet aphid fluid, honeydew, plant juices, and other insects	by rubbing its wings together	through its proboscis

Answers for game cards on page 76.

mostly other insects	to communicate and find mates	honeycomb (plug of wax to seal off the honey)	egg, larva, chrysalis, adult	the Queen bee
in colonies in a nest	six	nymph	nectar, tree sap, decaying fruits and animals	yes
they migrate to Mexico or to California	nocturnal	the Luna moth	red, yellow, and black coloring warns "not good to eat," camouflage, and "playing dead"	the dragon

The Cinderella Game

S—setting
H—hero
V—villain
SH—shoe
M—magic
P—party

Story Cards

Start

Free Choice

Interactive Projects & Displays © 2006 Creative Teaching Press

Water World

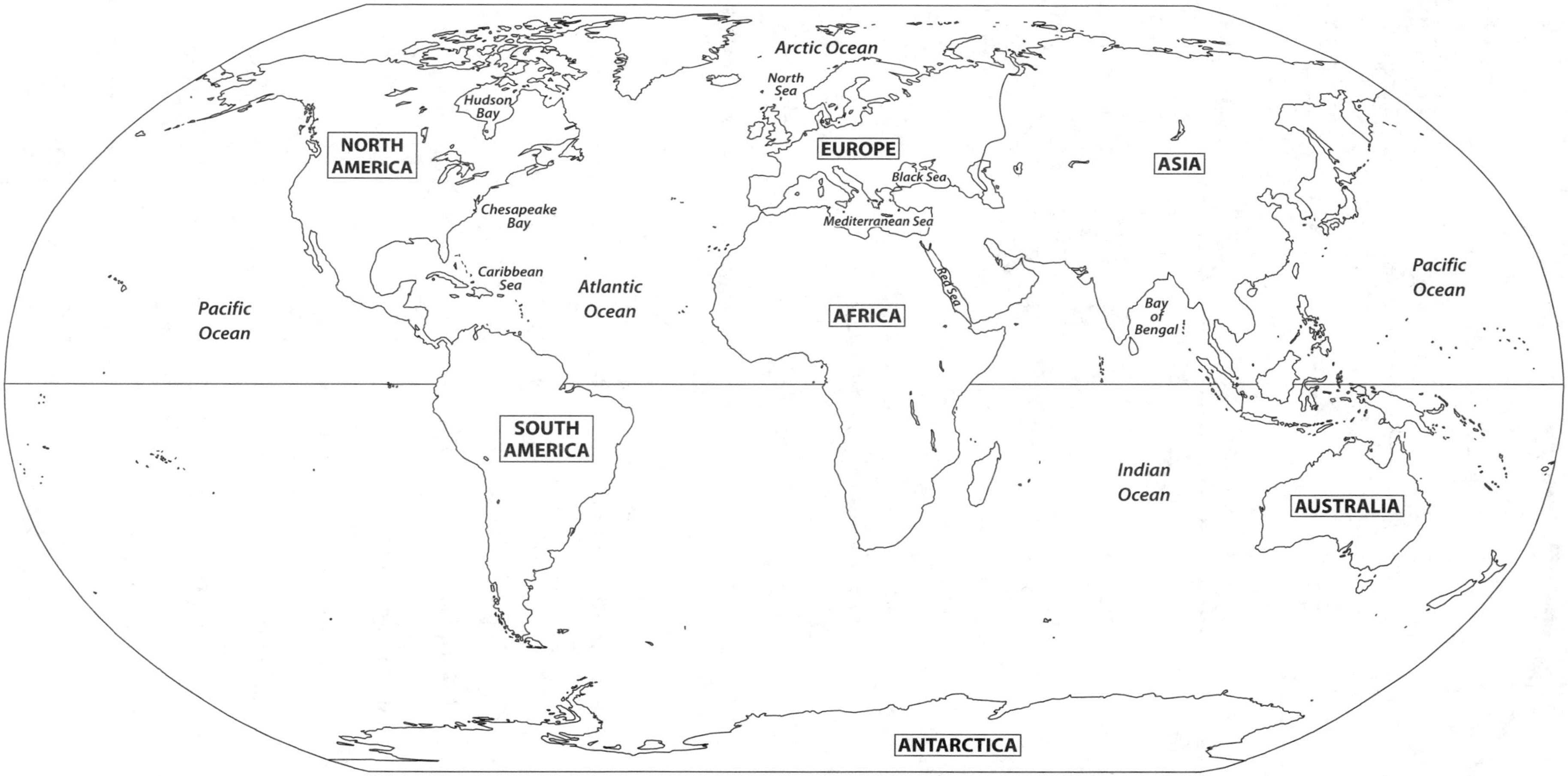

NORTH AMERICA

SOUTH AMERICA

EUROPE

ASIA

AFRICA

AUSTRALIA

ANTARCTICA

Pacific Ocean

Atlantic Ocean

Indian Ocean

Pacific Ocean

Arctic Ocean

Caribbean Sea

Chesapeake Bay

Hudson Bay

North Sea

Mediterranean Sea

Black Sea

Red Sea

Bay of Bengal

Blank Spinners

Directions

1 Label the sections.

2 Cut out the spinner.

3 Glue the spinner on 4" (10 cm) card stock backing.

4 Put a brass fastener through the end of a paper clip, and push the fastener through the center of the spinner.

Directions

1 Label the sections.

2 Cut out the spinner.

3 Glue the spinner on 5" (13 cm) square card stock backing.

4 Put a brass fastener through the end of a paper clip, and push the fastener through the center of the spinner.

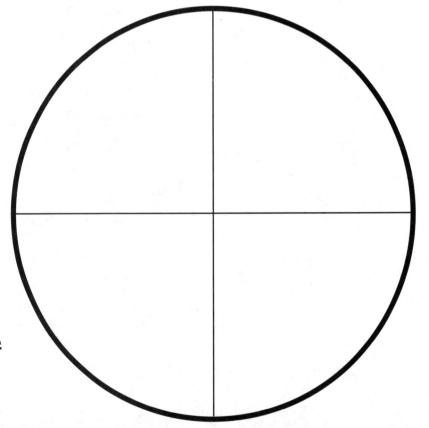